Y0-BCG-201

Donated to
Galveston College
Library

in memory of

Wayne Froeschl

by author

3-31-76.

DAVID GLENN HUNT
MEMORIAL LIBRARY
GALVESTON COLLEGE

Seeker

Dorothy Bettencourt Epston

Seeker

by Dorothy Bettencourt Elfstrom

Illustrations by Sharlee H. Holcomb

The Naylor Company
Book Publishers of the Southwest

San Antonio, Texas

DAVID GLENN HUNT
MEMORIAL LIBRARY
GALVESTON COLLEGE

Library of Congress Cataloging in Publication Data

Elfstrom, Dorothy Bettencourt, 1914-
    Seeker: [poems]

    I. Holcomb, Sharlee H. II. Title.
PS3555.L4S4   811'.5'4   75-9603
ISBN 0-8111-0563-6

Also by the author:

Challenge of the Seasons

Copyright ©, 1975 by DOROTHY BETTENCOURT ELFSTROM

This book or parts thereof may not be reproduced without written permission of the author except for customary privileges extended to the press and other reviewing agencies.

ALL RIGHTS RESERVED

Printed in the United States of America

Contents

of inspiration

of courage

of love

of truth

of wonder

Foreword

SEEKER is dedicated to those who are searching for the intangibles that complement the material world . . . with the dawn of every new day each of us embarks upon a venture seeking many different things — knowledge, love, serenity, success, fulfillment, and a spirit that is unfettered by the complexities of a busy life.

May you discover within these pages something you seek.

Acknowledgments

Grateful acknowledgment is given to the following publications in which certain of these poems have appeared: *Saturday Evening Post, Good Housekeeping, Radio Mirror, True Confessions,* the *Galveston Daily News,* the *Texas City Daily Sun,* the *Galveston Island Mirror, Our Special for Blind Women, The Bulletin Board, The Tower, Country Sounds of the Southwest, Scoop, The General Ledger, The Moody House, Galveston Gazette, The Port of Galveston, Food for Thought, Galveston* magazine, *Ideals, Guideposts, The First Baptist Church Herald* of Glendale, California, Maud O'Bryan's column, "In and About Town," (the New Orleans State Item) *Star Bulletin.*

My gratitude to the following radio and television readers for using some of these poems on the air: the late Sid Lasher (KHOU-TV), Ron Stone (Channel 2), Jerry Towan, Ted Malone, Don McNeill, Dee Walker, Meador Lowrey, and Bill Webb.

This book is also dedicated to two seekers who hold a special place in my life, my mother, Margaret Rowan Bettencourt and my father, Henry Joseph Bettencourt. It is with appreciation and gratitude that I give acknowledgment to them for a happy childhood. They taught me to be a seeker, and they supported my talent for writing with their loving attention, encouragement, and enthusiasm.

# of moments

you hold my hand —
and the world changes color

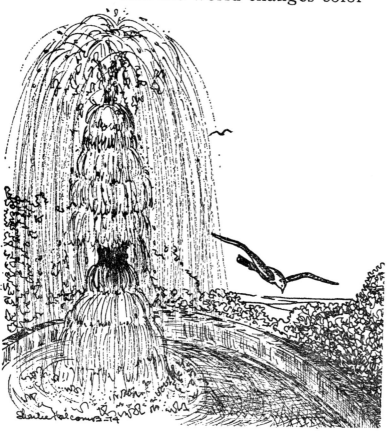

I'll Find You

I'll find you on a wintry day
In rainbows lending warmth to sky;
In firelight dancing on the hearth;
In pale plume clouds as they drift by.

I'll see you in a fountain's leap
To rise and fall in color flow,
Or sailboat silhouetted sky.
You're with me always where I go.

I'll find you on a summer beach . . .
In castles built of dreamer's sand.
I think of you — across the miles
I reach your heart and hold your hand.

With each remembered moment spent
In dreams that bring us face to face
You'll always be a part of me
For all of time — across all space.

Let My Love . . .

Let my love be young enough
To bring him spring's delight,
But also let it be mature
So I won't faint from fright

When he is late — imagining
A new romance has he.
Let my heart be wise enough
To know that he loves me.

Let my love be big enough
To share his hurt and sorrow,
With a reassuring strength
To help him face tomorrow.

Let my love inspire him
To dream and build and hope;
To know himself and live his life
In deeper, wider scope.

Let my love be young enough
To bring him spring's delight,
But let it be mature enough
To conquer blackest night.

"Farewell . . . with Love. . . ."

There were no words left to say
To tell what's in the heart. . .
Feelings too vague to convey
Kept pulling us apart.
Differences once bridged by just
The touch of loving hand . . .
Suddenly too wide . . . too deep
To fathom.
Understand that I do not love you less —
The reason that I go
Is rather than destroy the love
I must keep it so
That every moment that was "we"
Recalled in memory
Will ever be a part of me,
As you will always be.

◇   ◇   ◇

When a chapter of our life is finished, only memory
can bring it back to us.

I Know You

I know you —
 Not so much by the color of your eyes or the
contour of your face —
 The words that you say, or the words that
others say about you,
 But rather, by the way that I feel when I am
in your presence;
 For the me that you bring to the surface;
 The radiant me who is bursting with life and
love;
 The joyful me who wants to make everyone
else happy;
 The creative me who longs to improve the
world about us;
 The sensitive me who is attuned to the
needs and the hopes and dreams
 Of those around me, and those who are not;
 The me who is deeply touched by your
gentleness, your warmth, and your understanding,
 And who is aware of and responsive to your
moods . . . .

 These are the ways that I know you . . .
 The same as you know me.

Incomplete

The only heart I had to give
I gave away.
I'm sorry that it had to be
So late you came. . . . Today,
You see, there's none of me
To give to you,
And I would never offer love
That isn't whole and isn't true.
Maybe —
In some other time —
A miracle,
For some days I'm so lonely —
How I wish that I could love again . . .
And give you all my heart,
But I could never offer only part.

'Tis a lonely heart that has built a wall with no swing-
ing gate for a friendly call.

Once in a Blue Moon

Once in a blue moon
You meet someone
Who is unlike anyone else you have ever known;
Someone who is in complete harmony
With your thoughts and dreams;
Who knows the height of your joys and
The heartbreak of your disappointments;
Someone who shares the depth and warmth
Of your love and emotions.

Once in a blue moon
You meet someone
Whose presence brings
Delight, contentment
And peace;
Someone who leaves an indelible mark
Upon your life.

Once in a blue moon
You meet someone
And the heart joyously calls out . . .

Suddenly

Suddenly
The world was different . . .
A heart benumbed
By grief
And put to sleep
So that it need never hurt again

Awakened
And became aware
Of all the beauty
It had been missing.

Suddenly
For the first time
In what seemed an eternity
The splendor of the sunrise
Made the throat ache —

Fountains spellbound
The senses as they reached upward
In colorful streams
To greet the new day.

Suddenly
The whole world
Came alive —
Suddenly . . .
When you came along.

Unity

I hear your voice,
And deep within me
Begins to POUND, POUND, POUND
The restless ocean.

I feel the thundering urge of wings
Preparing to take flight.

I hear your voice,
And in my heart there echoes
Every song that was ever written —
Every sunrise beheld — and
Each love story ever told.
I hear your voice,
And I am ONE with all creation
Attuned to the
Author of Life.

Life is like the weaving of a tapestry — the dark
threads are necessary in order to see the light and to
achieve the perfect design.

There Is a You . . .

There is a you who no one knows but me —
A you who looks upon me tenderly;
Who is as gentle as a snowflake's touch —
The you who loves me deeply, and so much;

Who could not bear to see me hurt and so
Would guard me with your life from ruthless foe
Or unkind word you feel might make me sad,
Or anything indelicate or bad.

There is a you who talks with me of dreams
And all of life's exciting lovely schemes;
Of hopes and joys — and disappointments, too,
And little day-to-day things that we do.

There is a you whose precious heart I keep,
Who brings me love fulfilling and so deep;
A you whom no one else can ever share,
The you for whom I very deeply care.

Moments, like butterflies, are spectacular emergences of life.

Tranquilizer

Like a frolicking bear, the fog tumbled in . . .
Over and over and over . . . until it hugged every
    street.
The houses within this peaceful envelopment send out
    lights . . .
Guiding beacons . . . and tonight . . . when all have
    found their way home
The town will sleep in muffled embrace.

Vagabond

Whisperer of other lands;
Visitor of moonlit sands;
Venturer from far away,
I can feel your pulse today.
Vagabond of shore and sea,
In your song you speak to me —
Somehow I feel one with thee.

Communicate with Me

Communicate with me — don't shut me out
Of why you look at me with puzzled frown.
I cannot understand a shrug or pout . . .
Or silence. I don't want to let you down.

We are partners in this game of life, you know,
And if you will only let me try to share . . .
Sometimes at comprehending I am slow,
But I will listen to the dreams you dare.

Communicate with me . . . I promise you
The ties between us will be strong . . . and true.

Fleeting

He shall pass through your life but once —
The little boy whom God has lent to you for such
    a limited while. . . .
His passing will be swifter than you ever thought
    possible
When in future years you look back.
Examine every treasure that he brings to you . . .
The bird egg he just found — the horned frog . . .
The ring he presents so proudly. . . .
Listen to every adventure he shares with you,
For on one day he is your little boy,
But on the next day he will become your grown-up
    son . . .
And the little boy will be gone forever. . . .
You will miss him on every day thereafter
For the rest of your life.

14

# of freedom

Like a bird that soars o'er the
mountain heights

My spirit's free
when I am me

Teach Me to be Free

Jonathan Livingston Seagull,
Teach me to be like thee —
To soar to highest heights
And see things others cannot see.
Teach me to dare the difficult —
The unexplored and untried
And help me to gain the vision of
The potential that lies inside.

Oh, conqueror of thyself
And of life's sea —
Teach me to find the Jonathan in me
So that I, too, may know myself . . .
And set my spirit free.

How fenced in this world would be without our
dreams to set us free.

Love's Golden Treasures

When you remember me, please let it be
For happy moments that were ours to share,
Transcending from a weary world of care
Into another land where you and I
Escaped to let the busy world go by.

When you remember me, please let it be
Just as it always will for me —
A special dream forever set apart —
A treasured locket deep within your heart —
A place that no one else can ever touch
Where memory whispers, "I love you, oh, so much."

Two Lives

We lead two lives — the average bard;
One is a struggle, very hard
For bread; but not by bread alone
Do most men live. One life is known
By love and light the poet has shed
So man may have his dreams and bread.

When I'm with You

When I'm with you
I am a different me.
The me as restless as the sea
Sits at your feet.
Content is sweet.

When I'm with you
And you're with me
I am free to be me
Because I am complete.

How Will You Spend Today?

Will you worry and fret over yesterday
About words that you said or didn't say?
The things that you did, or didn't get done;
The battles you lost but could have won?
Mistakes you made and all that went wrong
Or greet your new day with a freedom song —
A song in your heart of faith and trust
That today will be better because it must,
For God loves you — He's your father and friend,
And this is His blessing — your day to spend!

Let My Child Be Happy

Let my child be happy,
Do not fill his mind with fears —
There is no need for gloom and tears.

Let his spirit soar.
Give him hours to play and dream —
For that is so important in life's scheme.

Let his heart find laughter
When I am not around to say.
Love him, but let him live
And be himself in his own way.

He is such a little fellow. . . .
He will watch your face,
So let him see you smile
And not find sorrow's trace.

Let my child be happy,
Give him all the love you can —
Unselfish, reassuring love
So he can grow to be a man.

Free At Last

God removed his outgrown shoes
And set his cramped feet free
To wander over hill and vale
Into eternity.

No longer able to explore
In shoes that bound too much —
Gossamer wings upon his heels
Now lend a magic touch.
God removed his outgrown shoes
To set his cramped feet free
So they might follow his young heart
Into eternity.

# of inspiration

the power that impels us beyond plateaus

The Lure of an Island

Like a beautiful maiden who is anticipating a rendezvous with her lover, the Island, caressed by gentle waves, excitedly awaits all who journey to her romantic shores. Adventurer, beachcomber, dreamer, intellectual, each seems to find in her a sense of identification with himself — in the joy of blending and belonging.

Bathed in moonlight and wearing blossoms in her hair, she presents an enticing silhouette. Her eyes are blue-green pools of warm waters that mirror lovely promises.

Standing barefoot in the sand, she teasingly warns that anyone who dares to get this delightful sand between his toes is destined to come back again.

There is an air of mystery about her and the lei of hundreds of fascinating seashells adorning her neck. Harbor lights are the glistening multi-colored stones encircling her fingers. Her hands are graceful fan-shaped palm branches that beckon and speak to all who are attuned to love and beauty, and who seek understanding.

Like the Madonna, there is an Aureole about her, but there is an air of magic too.

And one remembers always the warmth of her presence.

A smile speaks the same language in any country.

A Burning Candle

He snatched his dream and stuffed it in
A box, to let it die,
For it had broke his heart, and he
No longer wished to try.

He nailed the lid upon the box
And threw it in the sea.
Persistent waves dashed back to him
This dream that had to be.

He put a second cover on
And drove nails all around.
He took it to a desert waste
And placed it in the ground.

But then again, in vapor steam,
It seeped out in the still —
And he took back into his heart
This dream he could not kill.

TODAY is important! It is the FIRST day of your
FUTURE . . . and you can mould it into a significant
day of your past.

26

Masterpiece of Nature

Masterpiece of Nature, how you inspire me!
I cannot help but wonder as I'm looking out to sea
Where you've been . . . and if I toss you back, where
                                    you will go —
If you will live forever, and will you grow and grow?

Fascinating seashell, created to perfection,
Shall I take you home with me to add to my
                                    collection?
For now I find the animal once housed is not inside . . .
No need to leave your beauty in the beach sand
                                    here to hide. . . .
Dusk is turning into dark so let us get along —
The children will admire you, and they will love
                                    your song!

There are times when the most eloquent of words
cannot surpass the beauty of silence.

Sunset

There are those who have much time for dreaming.
May their dreams be good dreams
Not interspersed with nightmares
Of bad memories.

There are those who have much time for thinking.
May their thoughts be peaceful thoughts
Not invaded by reminders
That bring them regretful tears.

For it is never too late to turn from the past
And to look toward the future!

You

God has assigned a role to you
That He expects no one else to do.
Life is the stage where you will play,
And troopers who give their best each day
Till the curtain falls on the show's last run
Will know the joy of those words, "Well done."

If you really want to help someone, be a stepping
stone — not a leaning post.

28

What Can I Bring to My Job?

What can I bring to my job today? —
The will to work — a pleasant way —
The spirit to do what my boss has planned,
And a thankful heart there is work at hand.

Inspiration for the New Day

Watching the sun rise I can see
This lovely day was made for me —
The friendly sky — the fragrant air —
Nature beckons everywhere.
It's up to me to follow through
And do what I'm inspired to do
So that at nightfall I may find
A job well done . . . and peace of mind.

Poetry is the universal language of the soul.

Friends

There are friends, a joy forever
In the hearts of those they know,
And those happy ties will never sever
Though the years may swiftly come and go.

For those friends weave golden rays of sunshine
Through the clouds whenever they appear,
And though Life may turn their courses from mine
Their lovely presence is ever near.

The Christ Presence

It's good for us to meet someone like you,
With understanding boundless as the skies;
A friend we feel that we can relate to
And find the whole of living in his eyes.

With many we are often reticent;
To you we bare our thoughts, our fears, our dreams —
Your presence fills us with a deep content,
Releasing us from petty hurts and schemes.

What powers have you that set so wholly right
Our troubled hearts that sometimes get depressed
And rouse us to a greater strength to fight
Our battles with new courage — added zest?

We know you well, yet know you not at all —
And yet you make us see through Heaven's wall.

# of courage

the spirit to conquer

This Time

It's easy enough to give up the fight
When your luck is down and things aren't right.
It takes no grit to shrug and say,
"I didn't want it anyway —
It isn't worth the awful price —
The tears, the sweat, the sacrifice."

It's easy enough to admit defeat
And say, "Well, if . . . life *could* have been sweet . . .
I just didn't ever get the breaks —",
But if you have what it really takes
You'll make up your mind to get back in
And you'll say "This time I am going to win!"

◇ ◇ ◇

We are never so naked as when we have lost our
cloak of courage.

Be You

If you would attain your goal
Be the master of your soul.
Don't let those with selfish ends —
Posing relatives or friends
Rearrange your life — be YOU —
Unto your own self be true.

Those who love you from the heart
Won't desire to take you apart —
They find the artist in the man
Who wants to give the best you can
Of honest talent God inspires
With the kindling urge of fires.

Seek the truth and you will find
Joyful hours with peace of mind.

For each abandoned daydream plant a seed
That new may ever grow to fill the need.

Never Alone

I could not make today
Upon my own,
For obstacles along Life's way
Would get me down, alone.
But God is with me, and
The two of us combined
Can make today and all tomorrows
He may have in mind.

The Way
and the Light

The cross was heavy,
The way was dark.
Courage wore thin
Without Hope's spark.
About to give up,
Then someone said,
"Have you forgotten
Who is ahead?"

If You Let the World Go

If you let the world go as it is and don't dare
To do anything different, and if you don't care —
If you go about closing your eyes every day
To what needs to be done, saying, "There is
                    no way";
If you keep your mouth shut and don't try to advise
You may even be thought of as sober and wise,

And no one will say, "It's the usual story,
He champions the cause for his own personal glory."
Life will be smoother, with none to chastise
But the one in the mirror who looks in your eyes.

The duck is never apprehensive about the depth of
the water. Instinctively he knows that he won't get
in over his head. And if we live in Christ and Christ
lives in us, we can face the Sea of Life with the same
confident serenity.

"Be Still . . ."

"Be still . . ." and let your troubles float away
Like clouds — lie back and watch them as they go.
Awaken to the beauty of this day!
His radiant Love enfolds you in its glow.

Life's voyage is never ours to face alone;
Trust Him to guide the course and keep it true.
"Be as a child," He said. You are His own.
Be still . . . and know that He is there with you.

It is good that those in the world who delight in
putting their fellowman down are outnumbered by
those who derive happiness from building him up.

Stress is the foe that holds prisoner our thoughts —
stoops our shoulders — dwarfs our soul, and keeps
us from attaining full stature.

How Tall?

If there is a man
      to my liking in size,
He's the one not too big
      to apologize.
If there is another
      who is more pleasing yet
He's the man not too small
      to forgive and forget.

The pathway to failure is not as cluttered with mistakes as it is with misgivings.

There is no job in the world WITHOUT dignity — HOW MUCH depends upon the one performing the job.

The Uncontainable Charisma

They didn't understand him so they built a narrow
wall —
A means to keep him in the dark and held forever
small.
He didn't seem to notice though, and in his giant
might
He reached beyond their borders to seek the
broader light.

They fashioned him some guidelines — a puny
way to grow . . .
Beyond which they expected him not one step
more to go.
He didn't plead or argue — in quiet symmetry
He soared beyond their boundary into realms
they could not see.

Teardrops are like snowflakes . . . they go away . . .
But not before refreshing our weary world.

Worry is a tracing pencil that accentuates the hand-
writing on the wall.

A New Beginning

When problems seem to hem you in,
And there is no retreat,
Just close your eyes and wander down
To dreamers' happy street.

Whistle as you stroll along,
And see in your mind's eye
The faces of the ones you love . . .
Just let the world go by.

View the meadows and the trees
Or what delights you most.
Walk on down a little way
To find the sea-shelled coast.

Watch the waves come tossing in
With treasures for the shore.
Let them carry out your cares —
Begin a bright new score!

The fountain of youth could well be a pocketful of
stardust.

Worry will not keep tomorrow from dawning nor
bring back yesterday.

# of love

the essence of being

To My Child

My wish for you is not that you will be the most
successful
individual on earth but that you *will* be an individual.

Not that you will achieve great wordly power
but that
you will build up deep resources of inner strength.

And that whatever importance and influence
you attain
will be used in influencing others toward proper
perspective
of what is important.

"Spare the rod and spoil the child," some think is
right, but what I say is, "Spoil the rod and spare the
child, and tell him you love him every day."

43

Home Is a Hearth We Share

A house can never be a home
Until its atmosphere
Embraces love and friendliness
And people we hold dear.

Though it may seem a lovely dream —
Expensive and ornate,
A house won't be a happy place
Unless its swinging gate

Bids welcome to a hearth inside
Where everybody shares,
And anyone who happens by
Can feel that someone cares.

Love held lightly in the hand is usually the love that
lingers.
Love clutched tightly in the fist just may resist to
slip through fingers.

Of Home

Time goes swiftly — to their moms it seems
That sons remain as ageless little boys. . . .
She travels back to yesterday in dreams
When they were nearby playing with their toys.
She realizes life has much in store —
That each must seek the niche that sets him free;
In life's ongoing voyage — he must explore —
But she communicates by ESP
Her love for him, her constant thoughts and
prayers . . .
He is part of every joy the hearthstone shares.

It is astounding that something as fragile as love is
strong enough to hold two people together for a life-
time.

A Woman's Institution

She put a red heart on his desk made by her own
    small hand.
There was not a message, but she thought he
    would understand.
Too shy to even sign her name, she felt that he
    would know
How very much she loved him — but she
    didn't tell him so.
She found it lying on the ground where it dropped,
    perhaps a sign
A young lad doesn't think much of a heart for
    Valentine.
Today she took that same red heart to put
    beneath his plate.
Twenty years ago he didn't know he was
    destined to be her mate.

My love for you reflects in your eyes and echoes in
your laughter.

True Friend

He won't be among the applauding throng
Who court your smile when they know you are wrong
By word, or a silence you might construe
As favoring all that you say or do.

You will find he will dare to disagree
Though he knows your reaction is bound to be
An angry retort or a silent grudge.
But he cares enough to gently nudge
You to think things through to a clear, bright end —
He dares and he cares because he is your friend.

Reflections

For every friendship I have known —
Those passing through or those full-blown —
My life has taken on new glow
Which made me come to grow and know
God cares, for in each one I see
Reflections of His love for me.

The Heart Doesn't Feel
What the Eyes Never See

Grandmother said to me long, long ago,
"Don't question love, let it be.
Honey, be trusting — it has to be so —
The heart doesn't feel what the eyes never see.
Don't look for reasons to doubt the one you love;
Don't hear what others may say —
Believe in your love, and the good Lord above,
And you will be happy that way.
The heart doesn't feel what the eyes never see,
If it's true love is blind, then blind I must be."
Grandmother said to me long, long ago,
"Trust him, and he'll try to be
All that you're hoping, and you'll come to know
The heart doesn't feel what the eyes never see."

Marriage should not be used as a refuge from the
world but as a communion through which to grow.

Memo to a Little Boy

Charisma you have, and Nature has done
An interesting pattern for age almost one,
With your dad's flashing smile and his happy ways
And your mom's loving heart to gladden your days.
Others are waiting to find in you
Something of them that will burst forth too.
As for myself, let unfolding design
Dreams in your heart that will echo in mine.

Memo to Parents

Enjoy each golden day and what it brings.
Appreciate the dear and simple things —
Mornings that are bright with children's laughter;
Prayers at evening meals — the fun thereafter.
When these days pass, the heart though turned
to yearning
Must reconcile itself to no returning.

When She Is Needed

A mother knows that there will come a day
When trusting little hands that clasp her own
Will slowly loose their hold and slip away
Into life's pattern for the so-called grown.

But living always in a mother's heart
Are memories of each tender, growing year —
So special, and forever set apart,
When she could share each joy, and hurt and fear.

A mother shares, more quietly from the day,
Impatiently, her fledglings try their wings.
But she is always there, to help, some way,
When she is needed — when her young heart sings.

Time and tide wait for no man . . . but a woman will.

For a Special Dad on His Special Day

Dad's a great guy who must stay on his
toes;
Stand up to life's battles and all of
Fate's blows —
Appear to be brave though his boots may
be quaking,
For dads seldom cry though their hearts
may be breaking.
A friend who stands by us in all kinds of
weather,
Dad works very hard to keep family together
And because he is modest, we don't often
sing
Dad's praises that truly are fit for a king.

◊　◊　◊

Kindness comes easy to a loving heart.

To Each of My Children

If I could smooth the road for you
Along the path of life
And make your sky all clear and blue —
Your journey free from strife,

If I could fill each day that passed
With wisdom, love and beauty
And give you strength that far surpassed
Your every trial and duty,

If I could give you faith and hope
And courage beyond measure,
You know, my child, this lovely scope
Would be my greatest pleasure.

Yet know how deeply that I care
Enfolding you in love and prayer.

Happiness can be captured only by reaching out to others.

Essence of the Home

Grass-stained jeans with wearing knees
Nicked by fond, embracing trees;
Scientist with bug collection
Holds out hands for "washed" inspection;
Hears Dad counting up to ten —
Wagon left in driveway again.
Champion paste and paper waster;
Mom's official goodie taster;
Word repeater — heaven knows all —
Cookie and ice cream disposal;
Wide-eyed innocence and candor
On inquisitive meander.
Silencer of call to roam —
And love's fulfillment of a home.

Friendship: Each singing his own song but harmonizing in the medley of their beauty.

After the Ball

She met him at the Mardi Gras — a king behind
    masked face —
A fascinating one she saw of handsome poise
    and grace.
How glad she was when he came back
    so many times to dance.
He squeezed her hand — 'twas simply grand!
He liked her too — perchance?

The evening ended all too soon — the bright
    stars left the sky,
And she went home to face the gloom of
    Cinderellas . . . why
Do magically enchanting hours seem all too
    soon to flee?
"Mom, do you think one day that he will fall
    in love with me?"
"Who knows what's in the crystal ball?" — Mom's
    kind words soothed the ache,
For fifteen-year-old hearts may fall, but
    seldom ever break.

Love is the most beautiful possession we have to share.

Country Doctor

Time has run out for this great man of men
Whose heart was even bigger than his frame;
Who heeded duty's call, no matter when —
Who even from his sick bed rose and came.

Unselfishly, he gave his precious years.
Never by word or frown did he betray
The toll exacted of him, or the tears —
The weariness he knew along the way.

Your county sobs in sorrow, our dear friend,
We who loved you know not where to turn.
There are no other earthly hands that mend
And ease our pain as yours did — how we yearn

To hear again your gentle soothing voice
That melted troubles as the sun melts snow —
Psychologist, physician, friend, our choice —
That's why it is so hard to let you go.

We have searched for words and haven't found a one
That half expresses what we feel for you,
But when our Maker says, "Well done, my son,"
Our hearts will echo, "True — how very true."

Mother

Mother, there is none more dear in all the world to me;
Your sweetness, your kindness, and your generosity
Gave a meaning to my childhood that I'll treasure
    all my days;
Oh, the memories I harbor of your dear and
    loving ways!
I have never wished for riches, but this I have
    often said,
If I had a crown of diamonds, I would place it
    on your head.
Hardship hasn't made you bitter — only seasoned
    and more true,
And when God was giving mothers, I'm so glad
    He gave me you.

Love transcends all distance.

Mothers are the golden clasp that binds together the
volume of our childhood memories.

# of truth

the unalterable and ultimate reality

Quest for Truth

Our journey isn't easy as we go along life's way.
At times it's very hard to know just what to
do or say,
For our thinking gets befuddled in the trials
of the hour,
And a molehill seems a mountain to the
weary earthly plower.

The signs will then confuse us in our choice
of paths to take;
Little slights that should amuse us, much
too grave importance make.
Our vision becomes narrowed in the matter
close at hand —
We may make a wrong decision when we
don't understand.

Be our compass, Heavenly Father, to the Truth.
Along life's way
Let your Love and Wisdom guide us every
moment of the day.

Fortunate are they who seek truth and come upon it.

God Is Not Dead

God is not dead, and we must see
It isn't God who's dead but we
Who dare to say that on his own
Man comes to be — and stands alone.
Oh, foolish man who has outgrown
His Father's house; whose heart of stone
Denies the Love that gave him birth
And mocks the Mind sustaining earth,
Man big enough to conquer space
And yet too small to hold God's grace;
Sophisticated; so well-read —
Who still must learn God is not dead.

If each of us were able to reach the end of the rainbow,
we might be surprised to find that each was seeking
a different pot of gold.

The hour of reckoning is when all avenues of escape
have been cut off, and man comes face to face with
himself.

60

Progression

Every stone that stubbed my toe
On pathways leading toward my goal;
Every cloud that brought me woe
But helped to strengthen heart and soul;

Every wind that battered down
Castles I so love to build;
Every time that Fortune frowned
Upon the plans that I had willed

Let me know with pointed stress
The price and measure of success.

It is man's desire to get to the moon and over the
rainbow that keeps the world looking up.

We Can't Run Away

We can't run away from our conscience
No matter how hard we may try —
It was fashioned to last us a lifetime
Though at times we do wish it would die.

We may salve it some days with the ointment
Of reasoning, selfish and vain,
And for a brief spell we imagine all's well —
But suddenly it will be plain

As the nose on our face that it's useless,
And until we square up we'll be blue;
Our conscience is God's built-in compass
For a course that is steady and true.

Each of us has his particular strengths and weaknesses,
and they are not the same. He who strives to overcome
his own weaknesses and to recognize the strengths of
others has attained a mature approach toward the
experience of living.

To a Crane Caught on a High Wire Going Somewhere . . .

Where were you going, oh lovely thing?
How many miles did you have under wing?
How many days had you flown on high
Ever determined to conquer the sky?
Did anyone notice as you passed by?

Probably not, but now all stare,
Curious about your hanging there —
Wondering if they will be around
When your broken body falls to the ground.

Where were you going, oh lovely thing?
And is your brave spirit still on the wing?

◊　◊　◊

"Where there's a will there's a way . . ." provided it's God's will.

◊　◊　◊

The respect one has for his fellowman is usually in proportion to the respect that he has for himself.

Age Is Not a Time of Life

Age is not a time of life — it is a projection of mood. When we are happy and full of hope and expectation, we are younger than springtime. When we are bored, upset or defeated, we are older than autumn.

There have been yesterdays when we were older than we are today. There will be tomorrows when we are younger than we are this minute.

Lord, I know that
By the standards of the world
I am neither wealthy, good-looking,
Brilliant nor of great talent.
But when I make the most of what I am,
Inside me I feel
Rich, beautiful, appreciated . . .
And content.

Today is yesterday's tomorrow, tomorrow's yesterday, and eternity's present.

Happiness is a gift of heart.

Looking Back

Where did I leave the youth of yesterday —
The one enchanted with the world,
Who tuned in to each exciting moment of life?

The youth full of hopes and dreams
Dedicated to making the universe a better place
In which all may live . . .

The one who created an aura around those
encountered
And captivated them with empathy
And universal love . . .

The one I like to live with . . .
The one I long to see again . . .
The me I must recall. . . .

There are no blacker ashes than those gathered from
an expired illusion.

When the Chips Are Down . . .

When the chips are down is the time to tell
Where good friends are that you thought of well,
For they stand by with a helping hand
And a listening heart that will understand.
When the chips are down, there comes the day
When you know your friends by their kindly way.

God provides, and you know that He will
Through the friends who loved you and
      love you still —
When the chips are down. In a time of despair
How reassuring to know they care.

Man will more readily forgive you for stealing his
goods than for robbing him of his dignity.

The Dream

When you have struggled to reach the top
And feel that at last you may dare to stop;
When it's the day that your dream comes true,
You will be losing a part of you.
You will look back with a wistful glance
At the you always willing to take a chance —
The you who would never give up the try,
And who wouldn't permit your dream to die;
The one who surmounted the qualms and fears —
Who knew about sacrifice, sweat and tears.

You will look back with a wistful glance
At the you always daring to take the chance,
And strangely enough on that day it may seem
That you'd like to return to the you with the dream.

The person who agrees with you when he knows that
you are wrong could well be less than a friend.

End of Day

Sometimes I've had the feeling
As I watched the setting sun
That time was swiftly passing by
And soon it will be done.

As I stood there filled with reverence
For Nature's wondrous way
I asked myself the question,
What good have I done today?

To my less fortunate neighbor
Did I lend a helping hand?
Did I listen to his woes and
Really try to understand?

Have I reached a rung that's higher
On the ladder toward my goal?
Have I taken out a moment for
Communion with my soul?

Was I honest with my fellowman
And also with myself?
Did I admit when I was wrong,
Putting pride upon the shelf?

Have I been a friend to those I met
In the things I did and said?
And when tempted to speak sharply
Did I count to ten instead?

Did I take time out to laugh — to love —
To think — to see — to pray?
These are the thoughts that cross my mind
As I watch the dying day.

A reason often seems sound because it is to our liking.

What Really Counts

It isn't your background,
Religion or race,
Nor the physical look
Of your body or face.

It isn't your brainpower,
Your trials or woes,
And it cannot be bought by
Your friends or your foes.

It's not your possessions
Nor station in life,
Nor that of your parents,
Or husband or wife.

But the realization
That God is in you,
And it's whether or not
You will let God shine through.

God knows where we are needed, and He puts each of
us in the location and circumstance to fulfill that need.

70

# of wonder

adventures into fantasy

Can the wonder of a child, once gone,
be found again?

Wishing

Oh, to be a child again,
And fancy the dreams that a child dreams!
Wasn't it only yesterday when
Life was a round of enchanting schemes?

What could come up to the make-believe
Of the games we played and the books we read,
And the fantasies we would always weave
When the lights were dimmed and our prayers said?

Oh, to recapture a child's faith
With the sweet contentment that it brings;
Kings would exchange their empires for
A child's delight in the simple things!

Easter Bunny Night

On the night before Easter
Each meadow and lawn
Was bustling with bunnies
Who raced to beat dawn.

The grass became rainbows
Of all color eggs . . .
Some wearing gay bonnets
And standing on legs.

Paint brushes were moving
At such a high speed
I knew that these bunnies
Would soon be in need

Of a rest. Peter Rabbit
Then called "Carrot-break!"
Oh, the loud crunching noise
All those carrots can make!

"Back to work now!" said Peter.
"There's no time to waste —
To fill all those baskets
We need to make haste!"

When the last egg was painted
And everything done
Tired eyes of hid bunnies
Would peer at the fun.

74

Santa Is Real to Those Who Believe

Santa is real to those who believe,
And he will be through all of your life.
How good to become as a child again —
Away from the worry and strife,
Capturing all of the wonder and joy —
The magic of this time of year;
Watching the face of a small girl or boy
Who is waiting for dreams to appear.
Yes, Santa is real to those who believe
In their hearts, and the lucky who do
Are bound to see Santa, and they will perceive
All the goodness and love shining through.

Captured: One Leprechaun

Hello, little leprechaun, why did you not grow?
Grandma put out food for you each night — she
    told me so!
Lead me to the hiding place of treasures that
you know.

I promise I will never take a soul where you take me.
All I want to do is just to peek and let them be —
Treasures — all your treasures — I would
    really like to see!

Take me, little leprechaun, and I will let you go
Hide among the shamrocks so that you may
    eat and grow.
You *must* eat if you'd be big — Grandma told me so!

She Couldn't Believe Her Eyes

Cally Ann couldn't believe her eyes —
There was a rabbit of bigger size
Than any rabbit she had ever seen,
With straight up ears . . . would he be mean
To the smaller bunnies hopping about?
Would Cally Ann have to protest in shout?

No. He took out a huge paint brush.
"That is neat! Oh, Cally Ann hush,
The rabbit will hear you and go away.
Look at the pretty colors. Say,

He isn't painting eggs. Oh, my!
He's painting rainbows in the sky!"
"Hand me a carrot, please, to munch.
This is so yummy! Crunch — crunch — crunch."
"Quiet, Cally Ann, as you were taught —
Four pretty rainbows I have caught."

"Wake up, Cally Ann," Mother said,
"Wouldn't you like to hop out of bed
And go find out what the bunnies brought?"
"Where are the rainbows I just caught?"
Mother laughed. "Cally Ann, you have been
                              dreaming.
Rainbows? No wonder you were beaming!"

A Seahorse for Santa

Charles Henry wrote a letter
To the Northpole that did say,
"Dear Santa Claus, the weather here
Is balmier than May.

"When you get down to Galveston
There won't be any snow —
With beach sand coddling weary hooves
Your reindeer may not go.

"We've got a Seahorse for Santa —
We will have him standing by.
We children are waiting . . .
And Santa, you know why.

"We've got a Seahorse for Santa
From the Gulf of Mexico —
A Seahorse to take you
Where your reindeer may not go."

Santa came to Galveston
With a smile upon his face,
Where everyone basks in the sun —
Oh, what a lovely place!

His reindeer stretched out on the beach
And watched the waves roll in,
And Santa coaxed, but finally
He knew he couldn't win.

There was a Seahorse for Santa,
Oh, this was something new!
There was no time to dawdle
With all he had to do.

A Seahorse for Santa
Who took him on his way,
And he will long remember
That Seahorse Christmas Day.

A Valentine Heart for a Snowman

They fashioned a snowman beside the oak tree —
And a likable fellow he turned out to be,
With huge charcoal eyes and a very wide grin,
But something was missing way deep down within,
For his eyes didn't smile, and faked was his grin —
Yes, something was missing way deep down within.

Then Cookie said, "Why not let's give him a heart?
It seems to me that is his missing part."
So they opened his chest, and they tucked inside
Their Valentine heart. "My, oh my," he cried,
"What in the world has come over me?
I feel as bubbly as I can be!"

"Now YOU have a heart," Cookie told the snowman,
"Now YOU can feel love the way humans can."
The snowman said, "Gee, this is all mighty fine.
Say, Cookie, will you be my Valentine?"

A rainbow is the eye-catching multicolored shawl the
sky puts on after she has had her cry.

Dear Peter Rabbit:

May I please go with you
This Easter Bunny night?
When you are hopping fences
I'll hold your neck real tight.

I'm not so very heavy —
It sure would be a thrill
If I could travel with you
To Peter Rabbitville

To meet the other bunnies
And get in on the fun.
I wonder if they'd let me help
If they are not all done.

I'd like to make a space egg
To send up to the moon.
I'd let ole Snoopy guide it —
I hope you will be here soon!

I saved you crunchy lettuce
From my salad plate
So hurry, Peter Rabbit,
Todd August can hardly wait!

Bimbo

'Twas the big night for Santa
And all through the town
Not a creature was stirring
But Bimbo, the clown.

In the rush of the day
He slipped out of the store.
Now he couldn't get in —
They had locked up the door.

It was so dark and cold —
He was scared and alone.
Then he heard Santa talking
In deep, jolly tone.

"Well, hello there, Bimbo —
What happened to you?
Don't you know that your brown
    eyes
Should never be blue?

"Oh, my! You are lost?
Well, hop into my sleigh.
Come, Dancer and Prancer,
Away, Boys, Away."

As they sped through the night
Santa worked at top pace.
To beat dawn and the children
Was always a race.

Then he came to the Baileys'
Where Randy lay dreaming.
Santa said, "Almost two —
When he wakes he'll be beaming."

Bimbo nodded his head —
Then he closed weary eyes.
He awakened on Christmas
In happy surprise,

For Randy was laughing
And tickling his nose,
And now Randy takes Bimbo
Wherever he goes.

The Picture Window Egg

There was once an Easter bunny who
Decided to create something new —
An egg with a window to look into.

So he moulded the biggest egg he could
Of sparkly sugar — yummy good!
Now what for the hollow? It really should

Be something for Bunny Hall of Fame —
Something to make the kids exclaim —
This was more fun than a carrot game!

But he sure did wish he could whistle a tune
When the lighting changed from sun to moon.
Would he give up? No! Never that soon,

So he hopped along, but he couldn't find
What in his Easter bunny mind
Was the object perfectly designed.

He thought that he might lie down for a spell —
Sleepy? Yes! A few winks? Well —
He would be up before dawn in the dell.

He did awake with dismayed, "Oh, my's!"
For the sun shone right in his big pink eyes.
Hurry! Or there would be no surprise!

He got there just in time, it seemed,
To solve it in the way he had dreamed.
When the kids saw HIM in the egg, they screamed

With delight. Of course, they didn't know
That a real live bunny was stealing the show.
Golly, he hoped they would hurry and go —

He had held his breath till he thought he would pop,
But the kids seemed glued to the candy shop.
Then an idea dawned — the bunny hop!

He stepped right out of the egg and wow!
The kids were really excited now!
Did the bunny hop, then he took a bow.

Happy as a bear in a honey keg
Was that Easter bunny in his picture window egg!

Inside the Panorama Egg

"This panorama egg is so tall and so wide!
I'll open its window and step right inside!
Don't bump your head, Randy — there,
    now you are in.
Who's staring at me with that funny old grin?
Oh, no, it can't be — it *is* Peter Cottontail
Who came hopping along. Is this Bunny Trail?
I'll follow behind him to see where he goes.
This trail is real fine! Longer — longer it grows.
I'll sit here and rest while Peter eats clover —
I wonder if all of his freinds will be over.

"There's little Chick Chick — how are you today?
Come talk to Randy — oh, don't run away.
Here is your mother. Hello, Mamma Hen —
I haven't seen you since I don't know when.
Quack, quacking duck, you make so much noise —
Are you a friend to all good little boys?
Oh, there's Bugs Bunny! I feel like a speck!
If you will bend down, I'll climb up on your neck.
It's real high up here — ooh — don't let me fall —
I sure didn't know, Bugs, that you were this tall!

"Hop softly, please — there are eggs all around.
They seem to be popping up out of the ground!
Would anyone mind if I take some for me?
Such pretty colors I never did see —
Dipped in the rainbow and dried in the sun.
Don't think I ever have had this much fun!

86

Please turn around, Bugs Bunny —
I must get home —
Mom's saying, 'Randy, where did you roam?
My! How enchanting your dream seemed to be!
That's what's so nice about being just three!' "

Easter Treasures

"Stay here, little bunny," big Jack Rabbit said,
"We must get along — there is much work ahead.
With your tiny legs, you could never keep up,
Especially should we run into a pup."
So they dashed on their way and left Thumper to gaze
Into the store window of Easter displays.

He blinked his pink eyes that were ready to close,
But this was exciting, and he must not doze!
Eggs of all colors were there in the green —
A panorama egg! Biggest he'd ever seen!

Inside a ballerina, waiting to dance,
If he asked her, he wondered, would she perchance?
As if she had heard, she stepped out of the egg,
And on tiptoe she whirled till he thought he
        should beg
Her to stop, or could be, much to her sorrow
She would be tired come Easter tomorrow.

Then Brer Rabbit said, "Here's the all-rabbit band
With 'The Easter Parade' — let's give them a hand."
The cottontails waltzed in their new suits and dresses.
"Look who has arrived," said Brer Rabbit,
        "Three guesses.
It's Peter Cottontail and his lady devout,
Who wears a gay bonnet with ears peeping out."

Thumper heard a voice saying, "Wake up, little one!
Almost morning — we'll hide and peek out
at the fun!"
Thumper rubbed his pink eyes — he had
fallen asleep.
Oh, the sweet happy dreams that were all his to keep.

89

Mischievous March Wind

The wind is a mischievous boy today
Going home from school, in the mood for play;
He lifts the tresses of ruffled girls
And lets them fall in tangled swirls.

He takes a hat from a cocky head
And carries it off to a muddy bed;
He roars at the plants beginning to flower
And frightens them till they cringe and cower.

But then — after all day's gadding about,
Twilight comes, and he's tuckered out,
And Mother Earth, understandingly,
Lulls him into tranquility.

Pumpkins Are Jack-O'-Lanterns At Heart

Mr. Pumpkin, growing there,
You seem not to have a care,
But I hear your pleading heart:

"Please — please don't take me apart —
I would not be good for pies,
Let the children carve me eyes —
Eyes to see the witches fly
On their broomsticks in the sky —
Ghosts and goblins by the dozens
Coming home to visit cousins.

"Maybe they will carve me ears:
Lucky is the one who hears
Black cats 'Meow' and owls say, 'Who-oo-o';
Scarecrows shouting, 'Shoo, bat, shoo!'
Halloween is dark and dreary —
I would make a glow that's cheery.
I would like some teeth to eat
Spicy doughnuts, sugar sweet;
Teeth to bob for and to chew
Apples, later glazed with goo.

"Carve me out so all may see
Pumpkin Jack-o'-lantern me."

Mr. Bones

I'm the victim of diet, as you can see —
The worms are fat, and my bones are free.
They crunched and munched till I was bare
And left me to shiver in frosty air.
It's fun to hear children shout, "Oh, my!"
As they see me dangling, but no brave guy
Has offered as yet to take me along,
Or play on my ribs the skeleton song.
So I'll just hang around this ghostful scene
And wish you a "Boney" Halloween.

A Boy and a Bear

He looked a bit sad in the window downtown,
But the crowd rushed on by without heeding the
    brown
Eyes that said, "Take me home — won't somebody
    please?
I have waited so long for a big friendly squeeze."

Then there came a young man not much over two
Whose gaze met those eyes with his wide eyes of blue.
Though his mother's hand tugged at the boy's little
    hand,
The boy seemed to know that she did understand,

For Bill soon held the bear. Said the storeman so tall,
"Quite an armful of love for a fellow that small!"

92

First Halloween

On Thursday night when the ghosts are out,
And the owls ask, "Who?" as the goblins shout;
When the witches dance and their mischief brew,
And the flying bats are out pranking too
Trying to tangle the children's hair;
When skeletons shake and black cats stare —

If a blue-eyed ghost you should happen to meet
Who is yet too young to say, "Trick or Treat,"
But who offers his hand to let you know
He would like a treat. In the pumpkin glow
That mischievous smile like you've never seen
Will be Ghost Charles Henry at his first Halloween.

Valentineville

Have you ever ventured to Valentineville?
It's over the rainbow atop Cupid's Hill.
Hearts point the way as they frolic along,
And tiny red birds chirp a happiness song.
Chipmunks are hiding in marshmallow trees,
And little signs read, "Be my Valentine — please."
The streets are rock candy — red, shiny and narrow,
Where Cupid makes magic with true bow and arrow.

Have you ever ventured to Valentineville?
If you haven't you're missing a most happy thrill!

93

Scampi

Scampi, the squirrel, is my fine furry friend —
I watch him each day when he comes round the bend
Of the old pecan tree in our shady backyard.
He pretends not to see me, and he works very hard
Gathering nuts for the winter as if they were gold. . . .
Seems he knows icy branches get barren and cold,
So wisely he hastens to fill up his nest. . . .
Scampi is pleased, somehow knowing he's blessed.
He explores every branch, moving gracefully along,
And I feel in his presence a happiness song.
Scampi's one of my busiest, most peaceful friends. . . .
Though it seems he's not watching, he only pretends.

Winner?*

Buddy Boy is just a bull to others —
Some look down their noses at my friend,
But Buddy Boy and I have had many a cry —
It grieves me that our friendship now may end.

Buddy Boy is almost like my brother —
Through all those months I knew this day would
come.
The sadness in his eyes lets me know it's no surprise
To Buddy Boy — believe me, he's not dumb.

Tonight I lie beside him for the last time?
I think of all the romping and the fun.
I can't believe the time has gone so swiftly . . .
Lord help me face tomorrow when it's done.

*This poem was written about an entry in the Fat
Stock Show competition and his owner, a boy who
realizes that the loser may be his to keep . . . and
the winner will be gone forever. . . .

A Story About a Galveston Frog

A frog he did a flyin' go,
Oh ho, oh ho,
A frog he did a flyin' go —
His pa said, "Son, go see some snow,"
Oh ho, oh ho.

That frog was born in Galveston —
Palm trees, warm breeze —
That frog was born in Galveston,
But his pa said, "Look here, my son,
Find snow-topped trees.

"I never did get off this Isle,
Oh no, oh no,
I never did get off this Isle,
And if you want your pa to smile
Please go — see snow."

He hopped a plane,
And away that frog did go,
Oh ho,
He hopped a plane, and he did go
Way up north to Ohio,
Hi ho, hi ho.

But when he saw those banks of snow,
He felt so low.
When he saw those banks of snow,
He said, "This ain't for me, I know,
Oh no, oh no."

And back he flew to Galveston — no pause;
He was
A frog who loves his Galveston,
The seashore, and the nice warm sun —
But snow? Oh no!

The Mysterious Neptune Bunny

A mysterious rabbit rose out of the sea —
A Neptune Bunny he turned out to be
With shimmering coat of bluish-green . . .
The prettiest rabbit I'd ever seen.

I stared until I was hypnotized and
Under the spell of his searching eyes.
"Why are you here?" I managed to say. . . .
"Oh, I bring you treasures for Easter Day."

He offered a sack made from seaweed to me
With scores of treasures delightful to see.
"Take each one up and listen well,
For all have adventuresome stories to tell."

Then Mother's voice called, "Wake up, Henry . . .
    it's late!"
So I didn't find out Neptune Bunny's fate,
But again today after school I'll go
Down to the beach for somehow I know
That Neptune Bunny is coming back. . . .
I can see him now with his treasure sack.